H. O. P. E.
Helping Others Progress Efficiently

H. O. P. E.
Helping Others Progress Efficiently

Khaleel Siddiq

J. Kenkade
PUBLISHING

Bryant, Arkansas

HOPE: Helping Others Progress Efficiently

Copyright © 2023 by Khaleel Siddiq

All rights reserved. No part of this book may be photocopied, reproduced, distributed, uploaded, or transmitted in any form or by any means, or stored in a database or retrieval system, without the prior written permission of the publisher.

J. Kenkade Publishing
5920 Highway 5 N. Ste. 7
Bryant, AR 72022
www.jkenkadepublishing.com
Social Media: @jkenkadepublishing

J. Kenkade Publishing is a registered trademark.

Printed in the United States of America
ISBN 978-1-955186-52-0

The views expressed in this book are those of the author and do not necessarily reflect the views of Publisher.

Khaleel Siddiq

A Book of Quotes

HOPE: *Helping Others Progress Efficiently*

We can walk on water or drown while thinking we can't. We can move these mountains or procrastinate, while thinking we can't. We can overcome these barriers or remain stagnant while thinking we can't. For whatever reasons we have for thinking that we can't or that the struggle is just too severe to get through or to handle, there are a billion solutions that say we can. It's not about the problems, it's about the person that the problem or problems are addressing. We are more than equipped to address these problems/struggles, which results in a solution best fit for our lives.

❖

When life seems to be unbalanced, just stick around, and hang in there you know? Doing so will balance out but we must be strong, believe, and endure the hardships of life. We must turn them into something healthy that can benefit our mind, our heart, and soul. This is Khaleel. I hope that you can understand me.

❖

We have to deprogram and reprogram for the sake of consciousness and truth. There is a system set in place, a system that targets the mind. A system that effects the actions of an individual. The path doesn't discriminate against those who are upon it, but eliminates those upon it, and stages on up to the final elimination. If we continue to live unconscious; to live without truth, we will set our own selves up for elimination, causing a lot at this very present moment from the mind state to actions. This is Khaleel. If you don't care, at least make sure the youth do so that they don't have to experience those struggles or go down those dark paths.

Khaleel Siddiq

Swimming in water is the beginning process to understanding the dynamics of water, so that you can be able to walk on it! We can be fully emerged in faith, but it means very little unless we can walk on that same faith. I'm not talking about religion, I'm talking about the ability to turn "I can't" into "I can." I'm talking about the ability to be able to reconstruct a struggle and turn it into a steppingstone. I'm talking about the ability to rise and become a solution in a world or community filled with problems, pain, and persecution. This is Khaleel. Keep it strong and keep moving along. #mindovermatter.

HOPE: *Helping Others Progress Efficiently*

❧

The struggle doesn't stop, and we must prepare (but not dwell in our readiness) to deal with a struggle in a way that we are sad or depressed because we know it's coming. Instead, be ready in a way that whenever it approaches our doorstep, we have anticipated it's coming. Therefore, we can respond with wisdom and intelligence, and come out a victor. This is Khaleel. #itsalwaysgonebesomething

We have to believe! Believe what? Believe that we are winners and that we have already won. I don't know about you, but I'm going all in! This is Khaleel. You can get with the program or create your own. The choice is ours, the power we possess.

It's not that they don't believe you or understand you, they want to see the fruits from where you have planted that seed before they plant there themselves! It might make (sense) but does it make (cents)? What are the benefits? What are the pros and cons? What are the side effects? It's ok to talk to the people but sometimes you must show them to enroll them. This is Khaleel. It isn't anything but an opportunity and I'm gon' show you what to do with it.

Life is always teaching. Not just life, but our relationships with friends and family. Our encounters with people in public from stores, to parks, to our jobs and etc. They all hold valuable lessons and clues, and give off light in areas so that we can see and bear witness to the roles of people telling us who they are and how to go about dealing with them. We must be "woke" like we must be for work and to eat. This is for the conscious minds because we have to be "woke" to understand it. It's knowledge but it's not what you have that counts, it's what you do with it.

HOPE: *Helping Others Progress Efficiently*

Class is in session! If we have D's and F's, it's because we are not tuned in to what's going on and why it's going on. That's why we hurt. That's why we struggle, but we're not supposed to struggle like that. We're not supposed to hurt like that, but we can get those grades up and reform what must be reformed. We can put protection on the things that should be protected like our hearts and minds, but we must attend class and play the role of a student. Not an absent student, because if we don't learn, then we burn and will continue to burn on down to nothing. We must wake up or burn while asleep in a house fire at a time you should've been up. This is Khaleel.

It's called the distraction wave! What is a distraction wave? A distraction wave is a wave meant to distract one from one's own potential, goals, and desires. The distraction wave is powerful enough to implement ignorance in the mind of a person, causing a person to speak abruptly and etc. It can also put a person in a state of fatigue at the same time. The distraction wave is merely a struggle that we face day after day. It just doesn't stop but we can stop ourselves from receiving the side effects of this natural distraction that comes from the everyday struggle, but only if we believe that we have what it takes to do so. This is Khaleel and I'm giving to those reading this book a message of power- a message of mental peace.

Regardless of the struggle or struggles we face It's not every day that there will be a storm but when it is, we have to weather it. Truth be told, as long as we live, the struggle will be amongst us. Good news is that we can overcome it and rise above it to an extent that the effects of the struggle are hardly felt. This is Khaleel and I hope that someone can hear me.

There's one tree that never stops developing and that's the tree within us as individuals. You know a tree by it's what? So as long as we are willing to grow, may the fruits that we bear be healthy and influential.

It's gon' take a lot longer when you're doing it and living it right, but eventually, life will begin to balance out as well as many aspects related to the human being. You just have to keep the faith and keep it strong because this isn't an ordinary song. We must find our groove, never lose our cool, and never play the fool. #randomthoughts #RandomPost Khaleel Siddiq

What's up world! This is Khaleel. I'm still kicking positive. I'm still kicking strong. I'm working on a new book. I know many of you will be excited because of this great news and many more will be excited to one day possess this great powerful influential book. This is Khaleel. This life is the final battlefield, and I'm fighting in it using my strongest weapon so that nothing unhealthy or harmful can prosper against me.

There are two types of people in this world. Believers and nonbelievers. I'm NOT talking about religion. I'm talking about those that believe in themselves and those that don't. Because regardless of where we are in life, we can go somewhere else in it. Wherever we want to! Up there, down there, over here, over there, it's up to us. This is Khaleel and I'm not dropping jewels, I'm giving them to you! #MAINTAIN& #progress

Khaleel Siddiq

The only thing I fear is failing in this life when I know that I have what it takes to be successful in it. I'm not striving to be perfect. I'm striving to make sure my good outweighs my wrongs.

HOPE: *Helping Others Progress Efficiently*

Prison didn't rehabilitate me but it asked me, "Do you want to be rehabilitated?"

Khaleel Siddiq

If you manage to get one foot out, don't call it a day, but know that you have made progress.

Any good that I do, I don't do for people. I do it for the benefit of my spirit.

It's time for something new, but I struggle with the old. It is a constant struggle, but I try my best. The plan is not to become a saint, but to not be much of a sinner.

All my hardships, all that pain that I endured gave me strength. It invigorated me.

Khaleel Siddiq

Prison was like college to me. I showed up to class everyday even when I didn't want to and because of that, I graduated on time.

If my life was a DVD player, it wouldn't have rewind on it, just pause, play, and forward.

I'm too strong to be weak and when I cry, I put my tears in a cup because I can't waste any water while being in the Sahara Desert. I have to survive, and I will survive no matter the environment or condition because I'm Khaleel and I'm strong. I will always be strong until it's over.

J. Kenkade
PUBLISHING

*From Manuscript
to Masterpiece*

Our Services
Author Retains Royalties & Rights

100% Royalties
Professional Proofreading
Copyright Registration
Online Self-Publishing Classes

For inquiries:
Website: www.jkenkadepublishing.com
Email: info@jkenkadepublishing.com

Also Available from J. Kenkade Publishing

ISBN: 978-1955186452
Visit www.amazon.com
Author: Khaleel Siddiq

Mind over Matter is the sequel to the author's first book, "Positive Quotes". It is filled with wisdom and words of inspiration from the author himself.

Also Available from J. Kenkade Publishing

ISBN: 978-1955186278
Visit www.amazon.com
Author: Khaleel Siddiq

This book is not just a book but is a book containing a key that if obtained through wisdom and understanding and by applying and believing in oneself to the utmost that one can believe, one can use this key to open doors that are not electronically monitored. This key is the most powerful weapon one can possess. This key is our mind. The author believes that our faith must be bigger than adversity. If not, then how can we overcome it? The author believes that life will teach us two things: strength and weakness.

Also Available from J. Kenkade Publishing

ISBN: 978-1-944486-04-4
Visit www.amazon.com
Author: Rahsaan Aki Taylor

A dose of inspiration for every day of your life. Each day, we are faced with challenges that we must conquer and overcome. The contents of this book will help you maintain, stay afloat, and solve some of your troubles. There is a skill, a strategy, and an art to living a prosperous and peaceful life.

www.ingramcontent.com/pod-product-compliance
Lightning Source LLC
Chambersburg PA
CBHW060904050426
42453CB00010B/1565